Empath

————— ❧❦❧❦❧ —————

How to Thrive in Life as a Highly Sensitive-
The Ultimate Guide to
Understanding and
Embracing Your Gift

Table of Contents

Introduction

This is the Ultimate Guide for the Empath – basically, everything you need to know to understand what being an empath means and how you can embrace being one. It includes the following:

- What empaths are

- Theories about empaths and psychic abilities

- The traits and abilities of empaths

- How to tell whether someone is an empath or not

- Empath self-test

- The pros and cons of being an empath

Introduction

- Common empath problems and how to solve them

- How to manage emotions

- How to consciously control empath abilities

- Psychic self-defense for empaths

- Psychic development for empaths

- Chakra development for empaths

- And more

If you are an empath or you know someone who is, reading this book and practicing the exercises mentioned here will go a long way into accepting the gift and maximizing its potential.

Although there are many books written about empaths, this book puts together all the valuable information and presents it in an easy-to-understand format so you can start applying them immediately.

FREE BONUS BOOK

As a Thank You for purchasing this book, we would like to offer you another book as a special bonus. It is called *"The Secrets Behind Subtle Psychology: Secrets To Getting All You Want"*.

This comprehensive book is for those who are interested in:

- Learning more about Human Psychology and how it works

- Becoming more effective in your conversations

- Improving your social skills

- Learning about NLP (Neuro-Linguistic Programming) and how to use it to your benefit

- Becoming more influential

- Learning more about persuasion, including embedded commands, law of reciprocity, the low ball strategy, and more...

So if you are interested in learning more about any of the above and also wants to receive updates and free giveaway chances on our future books, just go to http://bit.ly/subtlepsychology !

Chapter 1.

Understanding Empaths and Empathy

An empath is someone who knows what another being feels, oftentimes by feeling it himself or herself. The ability of an empath is empathy. The word "empathy" is commonly understood the ability to share feelings with others, but it takes a whole new meaning when empaths are discussed.

Everyone has the ability to imagine being in another person's situation. However, a genuine empath can experience what another feels even if he or she does not observe anything from that person or has no idea about what he/she's going

Chapter 1. Understanding Empaths and Empathy

through. This is because it involves clairsentience (psychic feeling) and intuition (knowing something without relying on logic or reason).

In other words, an empath gains information about someone else's inner state through paranormal ways. Normal ways to know someone else's emotions are observing body language and guessing what a person feels based on his/her circumstances. An empath does not need to do these.

Aside from being able to know things through inexplicable ways, an empath will often be correct when he/she senses something. In contrast, someone who is not really an empath commonly makes wrong judgments. Thus, you can tell whether a person is really an empath or not by considering how many times he/she was right about something that was hard to know.

Empaths are highly perceptive so they make accurate conclusions. Despite this, they may have problems trusting their intuitions, especially when they grew up being told that their gut feelings were not true. But if they push aside what they know, their hunches may haunt them until they confirm that it's true all along. When others notice empaths do this, they turn to them to seek advice.

Empaths may also be capable of projecting energy and emotions to the environment, to those around them, or to a specific person. As you may imagine, this can tempt some to manipulate others, but more often than not, they would only use their abilities to help. Those who can sense and direct energy usually become healers who genuinely care about their patients.

As you may have noticed, empaths are extraordinary. This is why they are often misunderstood. If you think that you or someone you know is an empath, you will understand empathy better by learning about psychic abilities.

Theories about Psychic Ability

Empathy, the skill of empaths, is considered as one kind of psychic ability. There are some theories that explain how psychic abilities work:

Electromagnetic Theory

Some people used to think that information travels through space like electromagnetic waves. There are those who also claimed that consciousness itself is a form of electromagnetism. They believed that psychics can receive information and "thought waves" that are broadcasted by their sources.

The electromagnetic theory is not generally accepted nowadays because it does not explain how psychic information seems to travel faster than light (which is impossible for electromagnetic waves) and why it's still intact even when sent from far away (electromagnetic waves gradually dissipate the further they go). Researchers also found no evidence that the mind exists as a form of electromagnetism. However, this theory is not totally debunked; it just needs more evidence to be considered as true.

Psi Dimension Theory

The psi dimension theory assumes the existence of multiple dimensions, which some physicists and mathematicians say is possible. It states that there is a dimension where consciousness exists – some theorists call this the psi dimension (psi means psychic ability). This dimension is in another realm so it does not follow the laws of the universe we are in, but it is believed to intersect with this universe at some points. If this theory is correct, it explains why psychics can know things even if such things are far away from them or in the distant past/future.

Chapter 1. Understanding Empaths and Empathy

Quantum Connection Theory

Quantum mechanics explores matter at the subatomic level, or at sizes that are smaller than the atom. At this level, matter behaves both like particles (solid stuff) and waves (energy), but it becomes a particle or wave based on what an observer decides to see.

This implies that consciousness has an effect on matter. When viewed at very high magnifications, matter can't be considered as real but only as a set of probabilities. As a consequence, researchers aren't sure if the existence of matter itself is real or imaginary at the core. To them, it seems as if consciousness somehow is involved in deciding whether things become real or not.

The quantum realm has laws that are so different from what we are used to that even those who have studied quantum mechanics are confused about them. For example, quantum entanglement gives particles the ability to affect one another even if they are miles apart from each other. This lead to a theory that everything is connected at the quantum level especially because everything came from one source (many scientists consider this origin as the Big Bang).

Some parapsychologists (psychic ability researchers) and consciousness researchers believe that the mind itself is a quantum phenomenon. They say that people can gather and send information via quantum entanglement of their minds with others' minds and with everything else. This is also a possible explanation for why some people can affect other people's minds and manifest a particular kind of reality.

So far, these are just guesses about how psychic abilities can exist. What is sure is that there are people who have them – such as the empaths.

Theories about Empaths

Empaths in particular are said to be the way they are because of the following:

Weak Boundaries

It is believed that emotions radiate from sources into the area around them. Empaths easily pick these emanations because their systems are calibrated to receive them, or because their boundaries are weaker than other people. In contrast, non-empaths are "dense" and preoccupied with their own thoughts and emotions. They may also have a stronger energetic shield around them that blocks subtle vibrations from entering their awareness.

Sensitive Auric Field

Empaths may have a high degree of sensitivity to what's inside their aura, which some say is the extension of the soul. Thus, if others' energies manage to enter their auric field, they will likewise feel it. This may also explain why they are sensitive to sensory stimuli.

Active chakras

Chakras are energy portals along the spine. Some believe that empaths have hyperactive chakras so they can perceive and release energies more readily. On the other hand, an empath is also in danger of depleted chakras because their personal energy tends to get drained easily (you'll learn why later).

Energy Links

Empaths may unintentionally form cords or energy links to those around them. This causes them to receive more input than others. Sometimes, they may do this with full awareness because they want to understand and sympathize. For them, being connected is just a natural way of life, and they don't really consider themselves as separate from those around them.

Traits of an Empath

An empath is sometimes considered as a highly sensitive person (HSP). This is partially true because being an HSP means being more sensitive to stimuli than most people. However, an empath's traits go far beyond hypersensitivity. Before discussing these, here is a test to confirm whether you are an empath or not.

Self-Test for Empaths

Answer the questions with a yes or no. Don't spend too much time on each number; just go with your automatic response.

- Are you easily overwhelmed? [Yes/No]

- Are you intolerant of noisy, chaotic environments? [Yes/No]

- Are you distressed by bright lights, strong smells, coarse fabrics, or loud sounds? [Yes/No]

- Do you get startled a lot? [Yes/No]

- Do you notice small changes around you or in other people quite easily? [Yes/No]

- Do you think that you have an extra-sensitive nervous system? [Yes/No]

- Do you easily detect whenever someone experiences a change of mood? [Yes/No]

- Do you constantly worry about how others feel? [Yes/No]

- Do other people's moods affect you a lot? [Yes/No]

Chapter 1. Understanding Empaths and Empathy

- Do you find yourself reflecting on things that others don't usually think about? [Yes/No]

- Are you conscientious? [Yes/No]

- When you are with others, do you know what to do to make others more comfortable? [Yes/No]

- Do you often crave to be alone after being with a lot of people? [Yes/No]

- Do you listen to your heart more than your head? [Yes/No]

- Do you cry easily? [Yes/No]

- Do you avoid violent, scary, or depressing shows? [Yes/No]

- Do you favor pleasant music, works of arts, scenes, tastes, scents, etc? [Yes/No]

- When you were young, did your parents or teacher describe you as sensitive or shy? [Yes/No]

- Do you plan your activities so you avoid situations that may upset you or anyone else? [Yes/No]

- Do you find it hard to be observed while you are doing something? [Yes/No]

- Are you highly aware of details and subtleties? [Yes/No]

- Do you frequently experience strong emotions? [Yes/No]

- Do you dislike confrontations immensely? [Yes/No]

- Are you told not to be too sensitive? [Yes/No]

Chapter 1. Understanding Empaths and Empathy

- Do you find it difficult to say no? [Yes/No]

- Do you often not say what you mean to avoid offending someone? [Yes/No]

- Do you notice mistakes faster than most people? [Yes/No]

- Are you quick to notice who is not being nice to others? [Yes/No]

- Do you prefer doing things alone? [Yes/No]

- Are you indecisive? [Yes/No]

- Are you a perfectionist? [Yes/No]

- Do you like thought provoking questions? [Yes/No]

- Do you know someone's emotional state without knowing why? [Yes/No]

- Do you feel energy coming from or being drained by someone or something? [Yes/No]

- Do you sense danger reliably? [Yes/No]

- Have you avoided harmful situations based on your gut feel? [Yes/No]

- Are you drawn to nature? [Yes/No]

- Do you love animals? [Yes/No]

- Do you feel others' pain as if it was your own? [Yes/No]

- Do you have a bigger perspective than others you know? [Yes/No]

- Do you hate crowds? [Yes/No]

All Yes answers count as an empath trait. The more you have, the more likely it is that you're an empath.

Living Life as an Empath

As mentioned, empaths are sometimes labeled as hypersensitive persons, but not all HSPs are empaths. They are similar to HSPs because they can be highly sensitive to sensory or emotional input. The main thing that differentiates empaths from others is their ability to gain information about somebody else's emotional state without relying on normal cues.

What distinguishes empaths from other psychics is that they are emotionally centered. They feel emotions more intensely, thus they are more responsive to emotions as well. When making decisions, they usually follow their heart, however, when they made mistakes, they tend to feel so bad about it that they may develop perfectionism.

Empaths are more than just emotional people – they literally absorb emotions of those near them. Sometimes, they can also perceive feelings of people who are far away when they unintentionally connect to them. When this happens, it can be confusing for empaths because there is nothing in the environment to explain why they are feeling the way they do.

Empaths need to distinguish their own feelings from others. They must develop a higher degree of self-awareness so they would not be overwhelmed by what they feel. When they learn how to do this, they can take advantage of their gift to learn what they need to know without being swept of their feet.

Empaths are highly intuitive and has a deep desire to understand. They have sharper than normal observation skills that enable them to comprehend things more. This also makes them more understanding of other people, thus they can be good counselors and healers. They can step into another person's shoes to gain a more balanced, more complete view of something. Others would go beyond knowing what a person feels but pinpoint the emotion's cause. They do

Chapter 1. Understanding Empaths and Empathy

this because they can easily sense whenever there are things going on beneath the surface. Because of this, they can be quite smart, and it is quite difficult to lie to an empath especially those who can read minds as well.

Empaths are often smart. They are curious about a lot of things and view diverse issues with an open mind. This makes them learn more than those that have a lot of biases. Sometimes, they would use their abilities to know more about a person and why he/she thinks that way so they can communicate better. There are also those who will telepathically link to someone else who knows a lot about the thing they are interested in – eventually, they become experts themselves.

They can provide valuable input because they can analyze well, calculate the pros and cons, and see one thing from various perspectives, but they need to be helped by someone else who are good with making decisions. They take a longer time to make decisions because they mind things that others ignore, such as the effect of their choice upon others and the possible outcomes.

Empaths are conscientious. They have concern over how others will be reacting. Thus, they are polite, well-mannered, and have likeable personalities. They are also likely to notice when someone else is not being conscientious.

Empaths have a greater sense of responsibility and justice. They can feel whenever people are wronged or in distress so they tend to become protectors. Unlike many people, empaths care about more things aside their personal interests. They strive to help others, even if they would not receive any direct benefit from doing so.

Empaths can't stand horror or violence even if fictional because of their empathy and emotional sensitivity. They cry more easily even from just watching a dramatic TV show. Because they can be emotional, they need to be in situations where they can cry or express what they feel without being embarrassed or scolded.

Chapter 1. Understanding Empaths and Empathy

Shyness among empaths may be caused by two things: being more sensitive and being different. Empaths can easily know what people really think about them even if they don't say anything. This can make them become self-conscious. Also, being unique can make them feel as if they don't belong. Sometimes, people tease them for not acting like everybody else, so they learn to keep things to themselves to avoid being ridiculed. This shyness is usually overcome as the empath learns that it's okay to be who he/she is.

Although one common trait among empaths is that they are shy, they can be extroverts as well. Empaths can be good team players because they think deeply and care about other members. They attract people who talk to them because they are good listeners. A lot ask for their advice because they understand people and their emotions.

Empaths can make people reflect upon themselves. Since empaths can feel others emotions (and sometimes thoughts) as if they are their own, they can talk about what's going on in a person's consciousness. Sometimes, they can read a person like an open book. When they tell what they can pick up from another person, he or she can self-reflect better.

Empaths are generally understanding of other people and their situations. They do not usually judge others because they can easily put themselves in their place, and they know the reasons why people are the way they are. Other than this, they tend to please people. They are friends with everyone and do not take sides. This may not be welcomed by some kinds of people though, and they can be misunderstood as being traitors or inauthentic.

Empaths sometimes have trouble knowing who they really are, because they have an intuitive sense of connection with everything and everyone around them. They take on others' joys and burdens easily as if they are one with them. When others are in trouble, they easily sympathize and find ways to help them. This makes them vulnerable to those who take advantage of their good nature. When this happens, they can be overly defensive and shut themselves off from others.

Empaths like to improve things. Many empaths are driven to create positive changes. Their inborn creativity, imagination, and resourcefulness help them to accomplish these. This is because they easily notice whenever something is wrong or there is something that is lacking. They want to help the needy and make life better for them.

Empaths are passionate. When empaths find something they care about, they pour all their heart to it. When they are taken away from their interests, they may become heart-broken.

Empaths can be burdened. When empaths do not understand their condition, they become overwhelmed. They may think that there's something wrong with them – this can make them feel depressed to the point of being suicidal. They may choose to be alone and avoid social interaction, causing them to be more misunderstood. Some escape their emotions by drinking too much or taking drugs. However, if they manage to handle their situation, they can gain immense inner strength that enables them to help everyone they encounter.

Empaths can lash out. Empaths are usually gentle creatures because of their natural ability to feel others' pain. There are times though that they can take in too much negativity that they can't help but release some of it. More often, they would choose to remove themselves so they would not harm anyone and they won't have to absorb more than they could take.

Empaths are often selfless. Sometimes, they are more aware of others' feelings more than their own. This makes them become less self-centered and more oriented towards others' wellbeing. They also have e need to take care of those around them. They are good listeners and can be very insightful counselors.

However, empaths can be narcissistic too. Although empaths are one of those who are more perceptive of others, they can sometimes fight against what they feel by developing narcissism. They may consider their gift as something that makes them more special than others. Doing this makes them feel more in control despite being greatly affected by those around them. They can also be more selfish because they feel as if others are draining them too much and they have to protect what is theirs.

On the other hand, narcissists can seem like empaths because of their ability to read people. The important difference between the two is that an empath tries to understand others to help them, while a narcissist does so to take advantage of them.

Although narcissists may seem thick-skinned, they are in fact vulnerable like the empaths. They only pretend that they are tough while empaths do not. Also, narcissists harm others when they are harmed. Empaths do not. They will change themselves to make their relationships more harmonious. Narcissists will just force everyone to be more agreeable to them.

The defining characteristic of narcissists is their overinflated egos. This is unusual among empaths because they consider themselves as equal to others. While narcissists do not hesitate stepping upon other people to get ahead in life, empaths will often consider how their actions affect others.

Narcissists may be sensitive to feelings like empaths, but while empaths will extend compassion, narcissists will be hostile when they experience others' discomfort. They do not bother to understand others' emotions but instead focus on ways to make themselves feel superior.

Chapter 1. Understanding Empaths and Empathy

There are those who consider empaths and narcissists as polar opposites, but many empaths can be empathic or narcissistic depending on the situation. Don't feel guilty if you think you are being narcissistic sometimes. It's possible that you are just protecting yourself from being drained that's why you became more self-centered than you usually are.

So, how did your test go? Did you recognize yourself or someone you know in the traits described above? The next part will explain just what the empath can do. After finishing this book, you will know how to maximize abilities that only empaths are gifted with.

Manifestations of Empath Abilities

Empaths manifest their abilities differently. There are those who intellectually know others' emotions while others feel the same thing. Some empaths sense emotions as a physical sensation – like heat, cold, electric shocks, and the like.

Many empaths pick up what another is feeling by being near that person. Some empaths are more sensitive to certain kinds of people because they are more receptive to them or can relate to them in some way. There are also empaths who can connect to animals or plants; sometimes, more than other humans.

Other empaths sense emotions in the air, such as in places where strong emotions were discharged. There are those who switch to another person's perspective when they watch the news, read something, touch someone's belongings, or simply think about someone.

Empaths' traits may change depending on a variety of factors, such as their own emotions, state of mind, relationship with others, and more. Thus, an empath can have varying experiences. However, an empath can learn to

Chapter 1. Understanding Empaths and Empathy

bring his/her abilities under conscious control to make his/her experiences more consistent.

Empaths can connect with others emotionally and intellectually. Emotionally, an empath may physically feel the emotions and subtle energies of others. This makes them more attuned to another's internal states. Intellectually, an empath may imagine himself or herself in somebody's place to understand the other more. This makes them more able to understand the other's perceptions, thoughts, and beliefs.

Some empaths have an ability to affect other people's realities because they can connect deeply. They can also have healing abilities because they can see energy and send healing energy towards where it is needed. Healer empaths may sometimes feel another's pain, but unlike the other person, he or she may know what to do to heal it.

Spiritual empaths may sense other people's connection to their god/s. They may help others to have a deeper spirituality as well. These people may eventually become spiritual leaders or members of the clergy.

Empaths may be precognitive and can predict other people's futures. They can become reliable oracle readers. But take note that not all fortunetellers are empaths. If one is an empath as well, he/she can read better because he/she will be able to sense information about the client that is missed by a reader who is not an empath.

There are empaths who connect more to animals and nature more than people. They can be excellent animal whisperers or gardeners. Some environmentalists and animal rights activists may be empaths.

Now that you understand empaths more fully, let's go to the next part of the book: trouble-shooting empath problems.

Chapter 2.

Empath-Related Problems and How to Overcome Them

Having empath abilities gives a person an interesting life. It turns a person into a superhero of a sort, but at the same time presents challenges that don't afflict non-empaths.

It may be tempting to give away these cursed "superpowers" to somebody else. Unfortunately, not only is it impossible, but rejecting them does not really help anyone. The first step towards coping is to acknowledge that you are an empath and to look at your situation objectively.

Pros and Cons of Being an Empath

Being an empath is not so bad; you just have to deal with some issues. Empathy is the ability to connect to a person at a deep level. This enables the empath to know what another is truly feeling even though he/she may be hiding or disguising it. This kind of understanding is valuable for those whose work involves relating to people, such as social workers, teachers, coaches, counselors, psychologists, nurses, therapists, managers, administrators, lawyers, detectives, salespeople, clergy, and the likes.

Empaths can potentially develop better relationships and solve problems because they can understand what people really feel. They can see through others' eyes instead of being stuck on their own perspectives. They feel the dynamics of a relationship so they know why things are how they are. Because they notice more than the average person, they may communicate better, be more influential, and fix more things.

There are downsides to this, though. There are some tasks and situations that need objectivity and not emotionality – empaths may have problems handling these. Making tough decisions that have a negative on impact on others is one of them.

Extra-sensitive empaths may be overwhelmed by the things they pick up. Because of the extra information, they may become indecisive and prone to mood swings. When they are regularly subjected to unpleasant or overstimulating moods, their physical and psychological health may suffer.

When they feel other people's pain intensely, they may suffer themselves and be unable to help. This frustrates them so much because they feel powerless, they feel guilty because they can't do anything, and they also feel the other party's misery of not receiving any help. Because of this,

Chapter 2. Empath-Related Problems and How to Overcome Them

empaths are encouraged to choose who to help, detach themselves from those they are helping so they can actually do something instead of be carried away by intense emotions.

Empaths may seek relief by escaping social situations and being alone, which they will benefit greatly from. Unfortunately, those who are close to them may not understand this need so they will prevent the empath from running away from them. Aside from this, they are judged harshly by society, especially one that does not know about empathy and other psychic traits. Sometimes, they numb the intensity of what they feel through mind-altering substances such as liquor and drugs – these may help temporarily but ultimately leave them in worse conditions.

The high sensitivity of empaths makes them catch what most people will miss. On the downside, they may become overwhelmed easily. Unless they find ways to manage how they respond to information and stimuli, they might become nervous wrecks and recluses.

Sometimes, empaths may be good mediums and clairvoyants. This makes them interesting to the spirit world. Because of this, they may attract both good and bad spirits. Unfortunately, some of these spirits may feed off on their energies because they have weak boundaries and they emit energies strongly.

In conclusion, being an empath gives one gifts and burdens. By learning to master the ability, you can use it to your advantage and lessen its inconveniences. The following chapters will deal with each issue thoroughly.

Chapter 3.

Psychic Self-Defense for Empaths

Empaths need to protect themselves because they can be sensitive to energies and entities that do not usually bother those who are not empaths or psychics. This chapter is about psychic self-defense measures. This is useful especially to those who are into the occult as well.

A disclaimer: the measures given in this chapter are fairly easy to do and won't take much time, but these may or may not work depending on what's actually happening.

When something's bothering you, investigate what's involved: are you having health issues? Do you need to talk with a counselor? Are you doing some things that are causing you harm? It's easy to confuse normal issues with paranormal ones. For best results, only use these measures as support. Get to the root cause of your problem and do something about it.

Shielding

Empaths are sometimes clairvoyant as well and can see subtle energies that are normally invisible. Whether you see energy or not, you can direct it with your will and imagination.

Shields are an example of things you can create out of your thoughts. You can use them to filter out unwanted emotions and vibes from other people. You may create a shield for several purposes:

- To increase your sense of security

- To reduce the level of stimulation that reaches you

- To ward off attacks

- To make yourself less noticeable to psychic vampires and black magicians

- To avoid being overwhelmed by emotions

An empath's aura has an outer layer that is thinner than those who are not empaths. It may have holes in it as well, thus the person is more easily influenced by other people and things in the environment.

These are some things that can weaken your auric shield:

- Injuries

- Trauma

- Addictions

Chapter 3. Psychic Self-Defense for Empaths

- Extreme emotions

- Permissions

To keep your shield intact, take care of your physical and psychological health. Meditate regularly to preserve your inner peace. Avoid giving permission to anyone or anything to ruin your auric shield.

Imagine a shield made of light and energy around your body. Visualize it as bright, clear, and solid. When you make a shield, you may clairvoyantly see it as having a particular color. You can keep this color or change it to something else. Good colors to use are gold or white. However, you can use your own color for as long as it represents protection for you.

Caution: some of those who use shields have reported that a shield only lasts for around 4 hours because it dissipates into the environment. Reconstruct your shield after 4 hours or when you feel its effects wear off.

Another thing you must remember is that you don't need to have a shield around with you at all times. If you want to connect with other people more, or if you want to feel something better, you can literally "lower your shields" to let in the energy. It's also perfectly fine not to use shields when you don't feel the need to have one up.

Get Help from a Friend

A friend can act as a living buffer of energy. If you feel as if you can't cope with the energies in a place or situation, ask a friend to stay next to you. His/her own aura may compensate for yours for the meantime. Interacting with another person can also distract you from whatever you're feeling.

Protective Tools

These are some physical items that are commonly used as psychic self-defense tools:

Mirror

A mirror is useful for deflecting negativity, especially when psychic attacks are intentionally directed to you. Get a small mirror and keep it in a pocket or wear it as a pendant with the reflective side facing away from your body. Intend that it will deflect attacks or unwanted energies aimed towards your person. Take note that this may work even if the person does not intentionally mean you harm, so use this only if you're sure that you won't be harming anyone you care about. The advantage of this technique is that you don't use your own energy to deflect attacks.

Crystals

Crystals can help absorb negative energies and give you protection and empowerment. Because they contain energy and have a sort of intelligence of their own, you can program them to perform simple functions such as disintegrating negative thought forms, alerting you of danger, deflecting harmful vibes, and the like.

A clear quartz crystal is an all-around amplifier of energy. You can program it to give you strength especially at times when you feel drained. To program, just talk to it in your mind or aloud and tell it what to do. If you think you have problems with a particular chakra (see chapter 5: chakra development), get a crystal that corresponds to that chakra.

You can also choose any crystal that you feel good holding. You don't have to follow the suggestions given in this book because they may have different effects on people. What's important is that you choose something that actually helps you.

Crystals have varying effects on empaths. There are many uses for crystals, but ultimately, you can program any crystal to do a specific function. However, there are some that are recommended for empaths because they are believed to have beneficial effects to them:

Quartz in general is an energy amplifier. Rose quartz in particular emanates love, so you can use it to counteract negative moods. Smoky quartz is a protection stone because it draws in negative energy and transmutes it into a pure form. It also helps with grounding.

Amber and black tourmaline absorbs negative energy. Having these stones will help lessen the negativities that your aura soaks up. You have to clean these crystals regularly though – if they get saturated, the energies may leak into the environment.

Onyx and black obsidian repel negative energy. The advantage of these is that they do not keep the bad energy, but they may launch it to someone accidentally. To prevent mishaps, instruct the crystal to transmute the energy into a positive form before deflecting it.

Red gemstones such as rubies, red jasper, and garnet tap into the root chakra and strengthen your sense of security.

Read more about crystals so you will have an idea of what may be best for your particular situation. Experiment with them by keeping it with you for about a week. Afterwards, look back and review what happened.

Salt Water

Water is an absorber of energy and salt is a purifier. If you feel psychically unclean, soak in a bath tub with salt water. You can also put it in a bowl and keep it near you. Just mix rock salt with clean water, preferably obtained from a natural source.

Cactus

A cactus can be programmed to destroy negative energy and thought forms in a place. It is said to emanate sharp energy needles that can puncture and disintegrate these unwanted vibes. Take care of the plant to show your appreciation for its help.

Amulets

You may wear an amulet or charm to protect yourself from energy vampires, psychic attacks, negative energies, and the like. These are available in occult shops. You can also turn any accessory into one. Just program it with your intention by saying it aloud or in your mind then charging it with energy (through visualizing energy entering it or by letting it soak the sunlight or moonlight).

Food

The food you eat may have greater effects on you if you're an empath since you react not only to its physical components but its energetic components as well. Thus, choose what you eat. It's better if the food is prepared humanely – slaughtered animals will leave food that is contaminated with negative emotions. You don't need to be vegetarian but it will greatly help decrease the amount of negative energies you consume. Eat healthy, stay away from junk and processed food, and drink a lot of clean water to keep yourself clean physically and energetically.

If it's hard for you to control your diet, try to bless your food at least. This will help erase the negativities you consume and imbue it with life-giving energies. Blessing can be in the form of a prayer, a request for the Divine to cleanse it, or a visualization of energy.

Avoiding Psychically Unclean People

People with a lot of issues may sometimes develop a tendency to emit unhealthy energies or deplete the energy of those around them. As an empath, you will be more vulnerable to these individuals. You may even have difficulty standing next to them or interacting with them over the phone or online. Do not spend a lot of time with them (whether physically or otherwise – energy can travel through connections) because it will be quite easy for them to penetrate your aura and feed off your vital energy since you already have a thin auric shield. If you can't avoid the person, protect yourself. Don't think that you are being heroic because you are "helping" the other person even if you end up depleted.

When these kinds of people give you something or touch your items, cleanse it. They may leave some energy residues or even thought forms or entities that will continue to deplete you even if they're not around. You will read more about cleansing later.

Dealing with Negative Entities

There are spirit entities that may become attracted to an empath because he/she has thin barriers, reacts strongly to stimuli, and can influence other people. Thus, they can attach themselves to the aura to leech off their energy and control them so they behave in ways that makes them generate more energy.

These entities may do this for varying reasons – one is to feed off energy by making the empath respond a certain way and another is to stop the empath from helping other people so they stop emitting negative vibrations, since empaths tend to help others become more positive.

As an example, there are entities that thrive on the emotional energy of anger. To acquire this energy, they inject thoughts and influence situations so that a person becomes angry. When they succeed, they will gather the energies that are generated. The more people affected, the bigger their meal.

Because of this, they will try to stop an empath or someone who is preventing the energies from being generated. Some say that this is one reason why empaths are prone to being distressed –

some entities are deliberately making them feel this way to hinder their efforts to help people.

It's easy to become angry at these parasitic entities for unfairly getting something that is not theirs and causing harm to you. However, you must know that you must not attack them because that will only give them more of the same energy they are trying to harvest from you. Being negative towards them will just boost their negativity and make them more capable of doing you harm.

Instead, send them the opposite of their energy. Bless them. Understand that they are just doing that because they just want to survive. Currently, they can't get energy from the Universe because they are not evolved enough. Sending them love and positivity may help them evolve so they would no longer resort to parasitic means to be okay.

Getting angry or fearful of them will just form cords that they can exploit. Forgiveness helps remove these unhealthy attachments. After all, we eat other beings to live, too.

From time to time, and especially when you seem drained or influenced by these creatures, cleanse your aura by emanating light from the center of your beings. Let this radiate outwards and imagine the beings falling away from your aura. Accompany this with emotions of love and serenity. Fill your mind with the most joyful and loving thoughts. Do not allow any negative sentiment to creep in to prevent these entities to hang on.

Remember that the spirit is indestructible and they can only be transformed. So don't think about harming or killing other spirit beings – it's impossible and doing so will just bring up feelings of hostility. Help them help themselves, instead. Raise their vibrations so they will no longer need to be parasitic. At the very least, radiating energy that is contrary to these beings' nature will make them leave you.

Cording

People create energetic links to one another. Clairvoyantly, they can be seen as actual cords – some of them very thin while others are thick and composed of many cords interwoven together. The more energy involved, the bigger the cords are. These cords enable energy to flow to and from the chakras of the people involved.

Symptoms of Cords

You will know that you have formed cords when you experience one or more of these:

- Obsessive thoughts

- Inability to let go

- Frequent conversations/arguments in your mind with someone

- Constantly remembering the person

- Being tempted to go back to an old, unhealthy relationship

- Stalking

- Negative feelings about past

- Wanting to take revenge

- Crying so much

- Disinterest in other people

Why Cut Cords

Cutting cords may seem like a drastic measure especially if you've grown fond of the person or object, but consider these benefits:

- To attain peace of mind

- To think more clearly

- To prevent being manipulated

- To increase freedom

- To be relieved of burdens

- To move on

- To avoid being depleted

- To stop hurting another

- To regain your energy

- To make the other person/being become independent

Who to cut cords with

You don't need to cut cords with people whom you genuinely care about and who feel the same way for you. For as long as the relationship is healthy and everyone is benefitting, the cords will help. Otherwise, severe cords with:

- Those who you're obsessed with

- Those who have bothered you

- Those who have abused you

- Those who you have abused

- Those you're attached/dependent to

- Those who you think are holding you back in some way

How to Cut Cords

You may call upon spirit guardians to help remove cords from your aura. Although the guides can remove cords and attachments without being instructed to, they usually respect your free will and will only do so when you ask them to.

You can try this prayer or create something similar:

"I ask my guides to help remove cords that bind me to (name of person)."

If you don't know who is attached to you in particular, just request that all unhelpful cords will be severed.

You can also ask that the energy that is taken from you will be given back, or unwelcome energy be sent back to the owner. If you don't want to harm the person, ask that the energy be converted into a beneficial form before it is sent to the origin. Remember, attacking tends to make things worse so seek a resolution instead.

When you have removed all attachments through visualization and changing your attitude, forgive the person/creature with all your heart. This may be difficult to do, but once you managed to, you can be assured that you have totally released the attachment and would not unintentionally send cords to the subject.

Reflect on the relationship. What lessons have you learned? Take this to heart and let it change you into a better person. Show gratitude for the lessons and affirm that the connection is no longer necessary. This will allow both of you to move on and learn new lessons.

Processing the relationship and letting go may release some toxic energies so you need to clean up afterwards. Relax your body and clear your mind of troublesome thoughts. Imagine a white or golden light sweeping your aura until it becomes clean and radiant.

When you are already satisfied with how your aura looks and feels, seal it off. Imagine fortifying the boundary of your aura so all holes, tears, and cracks are closed off. Affirm that your aura will let only positive energy in and let out negative energy.

Cleansing the Aura

An empath draws in energy from the environment to the point that he/she becomes saturated with all sorts of emotions and vibes. Because of this, it's recommended to practice regular cleansing of the absorbed energy.

Another way of aura cleansing aside from visualizing light is to create a connection with the earth so that you can "dump" the toxic energy in there. Don't worry that you will hurt the earth because the planet is big enough to handle it. It also has the ability to transform negative energy into positive just like it turns dead material into living organisms.

There are many other ways of clearing the energy, such as:

- Reiki

- Tai Chi/Qi Gong

- Meditation

- Psychotherapy

- Resolving issues

- Lifestyle changes

The main point of energy clearing is removing yourself of negative emotions. If you feel better and you think more clearly, it is a symptom that you have cleared your energy.

Replenishing Energy

Clearing out your aura can leave you drained so always replace the old, dirty energy with fresh, clean energy. It's better if you do this in an environment that has little pollution and a lot of plant life. You can also tap into the energy of the sun for this. Let the sun rays remove your unclean energy and at the same time give you new vitality. As much as possible, keep yourself healthy so you will have maximum access to energy.

Grounding

Grounding reconnects you to the strength and stability of the earth. This will make you less vulnerable to energetic influences. After working with energy, you must ground yourself so you will not feel light-headed and out of touch with reality.

A simple way to ground yourself is to eat something light. Walking barefoot or doing something physical is also recommended. For more grounding ideas, go to Chapter 5 and look for the section on the Root Chakra.

A more effective yet more challenging way to feel grounded is to resolve your issues. Anything that is left unresolved will make you feel uneasy until you come into terms with it. Once you do, though, you won't have to rely on superficial and temporary means to achieve stability.

Don't worry if you haven't completely resolved your problems yet, though. Just immerse yourself in something that you enjoy. Be with people you like. This should give you a feeling that you are safe and welcome – a sign that you have sufficiently grounded yourself.

Vacationing into Nature

Cities are filled with emotions that may overwhelm an empath. Going away from the city and staying in a place without much people will help the empath regain his/her stability. Nature does contain plants and animals that also have their own version of emotions, but these are often not intense as humans'. Plants are said to radiate a calming energy as well. When you or an empath you know is overloaded, go away from crowds and spend a few hours in a secluded nature spot. You can tap into the energy of nature to replenish yourself.

Clearing Negative Energy from Your Surroundings

Because you are more sensitive to energy, you will know easily whether a place or an environment will be good to you. The downside is that you will be affected by things that don't matter to others. For this, you need to clean the energy of your environment. This can be done through a lot of ways:

Visualization

Energy follows thought – this means that whatever you think and imagine will carry energy that will follow your instruction. Remove all thoughts from your mind for as much as you could. With eyes closed, intend to see the area within your mind's eye.

At this point, you may have an intuition of what to do. A spirit guide may also come in and give some instructions. If not, you can simply imagine negativities to be darkness, clouds, or whatever represents unclean energy to you. Visualize clearing these out with radiant light, a gentle breeze, purifying fire, or whatever cleansing method you want.

Smudging with Incense

Incense has long been used to purify a place. It will also leave the room smelling good, which will improve people's moods. Go with incense that appeals with you. Some suggestions are frankincense (traditionally used for purification), lavender (has calming properties), and sage (often used for mystic rituals).

Using Sound

Sound waves can push away unclean energies and entities from an area. Ringing a bell, chime, or singing bowl will emit a pure vibration that will repel anything that is impure. If you don't have these instruments, you may chant a mantra or play music that makes you feel peaceful and happy. In fact, some have played Disney songs to remove negative spirits from houses! Don't worry too much about the right song to play though. Anything will work for so long as it puts you in a pleasant state when you hear it.

Placing Bowls of Rock Salt on Crucial Areas

Rock salt has long been used for discouraging evil spirits from entering an area and for cleansing things or people that are believed to be contaminated by undesirable energy. Use rock salt because table salt is already processed and subjected to artificial chemicals and forces. The more natural the salt you get, the more charged with energy it is.

Put the bowls in areas where you sense something off. The doorway is a good spot because it will filter everyone and everything that passes through it. Another good area is underneath your bed as the negative energy you have accumulated during the day will be cleansed as you sleep.

Program the bowls with your intention. Imbuing it with your thoughts will make it more effective. Change the salt at least once a week to remove the dirty energy collected.

Physically Clean the Place

Physical things have an energetic counterpart. Cleaning the place not only makes it more comfortable and safe at the superficial level, it also improves its energetic quality. Because entities are attracted to energy that is similar to them, if your place is dirty, you may unknowingly invite dirty spirits too. Also, the condition of your place has effects on people around you, so make it easy for people to feel good by tidying up.

These should take care of most issues that deal with energies and entities. If you still need help, consider hiring a reliable psychic/mystic/occultist. Read reviews first so you know what to expect!

Chapter 4.

Consciously Controlling Empath Abilities

Being more familiar with empath skills will help you use it to your advantage rather than be knocked off every time the abilities kick in without your consent. Before anything, recall the times when you have manifested some form of empath ability. What happened? How did it feel like? What did you do? Recall as many details as you can and record these in a journal. When you pay more attention to your experiences, you will be more ready to control them.

Chapter 4. Consciously Controlling Empath Abilities

As an empath, you may have sent and received emotions and other psychic information without intending to. This time, you will do so deliberately. Before doing these exercises, you need to clear your mind of all thoughts and calm down all emotions. This will lead to more accurate results. Record everything that happens as well.

Sending and Receiving Emotions

Normally, emotions are easy telepathy targets because the subconscious mind (the psychic part of the mind) deals with emotions. As an empath, you will be more adept in receiving and interpreting feelings.

To hone your natural gift, you may practice deliberately sensing emotion with a partner. You may take turns being the sender and receiver of emotion.

The sender will spend some minutes in generating a strong feeling in himself or herself. This can be done by recalling experiences when the emotion occurred, imagining scenarios that provoke the feeling, or by visualizing concepts associated with it (example, darkness, scary noises, and running people can be linked with fear). The receiver will clear his/her mind and heart and wait until he/she feels something else. To help with the connection, the sender and receiver may imagine a tube connecting their hearts. The receiver will say what he/she received and guess the emotion.

Sending Emotions

Imagine your target. Feel his or her presence with your mind and being. Look at the target. If not present, pretend that he or she is in front of you. If you are targeting a group, see them around you. Have the intention of connecting with the target/s.

Chapter 4. Consciously Controlling Empath Abilities

Pick an emotion and make yourself feel it. Bring back memories or think of thoughts that will evoke the feeling. Let it fill your awareness.

When it has reached its peak strength and concentration, pass it on to your target/s. Ask the person or the group if they felt something and what particular emotion they experienced. Intensify the emotion, re-establish the connection, and send it again if they got the wrong result or if they did not feel anything.

When you're done, relax and ground yourself. Release all emotional energy.

Receiving Emotions

There are different ways to receiving emotions. One way is that you observe something from the target/s and this gives you ideas of what he/she is feeling. Another is that you don't see or hear anything from the target but you just know the emotions involved or you feel the emotion yourself.

When you select a target to receive emotions, it's better if you choose someone who you don't know much. If you practice with someone you know a lot, you may tend to rely on your previous experiences with that person to know what he/she may probably be feeling. On the other hand, receiving emotions from a stranger will leave you no choice but to rely on genuine psychic ability.

Calm all emotions first before reaching out to the target. Envision the target in front of you or around you. To lessen confusion, you can create a link that has a one-way flow of energy so you only receive and not send emotions.

Developing the Psychic Senses

Understanding psychic abilities will help you cope better with being an empath. Some associate empathy as a manifestation of an overactive heart or third eye chakra. Later on,

Chapter 4. Consciously Controlling Empath Abilities

you will learn how to work with chakras to control your abilities better.

Working with the chakras involves sensitizing yourself to subtle energies too. This is why developing your clairvoyance is a helpful (although unnecessary) part of managing life as an empath.

To develop your psychic abilities, you need to go into a mild trance so you can receive psychic information more easily. You must break away from your normal state of awareness so you won't confuse your imagination with what you pick up.

You enter a trance by doing the following:

- Relaxing your entire body

- Closing your eyes

- Minimizing sensory inputs (use a blindfold and earplugs, close your eyes, turn off music, go in a floatation tank, etc.)

- Taking deep, meditative breaths

- Releasing troublesome thoughts and emotions

- Keeping your mind as blank as possible

There are certain situations when you enter a trance normally:

- Before going to sleep

- Right after you wake up

- Relaxing

- Praying

- Meditating

- Dreaming

You will know that you have entered a trance when your attention is focused inwardly rather than what goes on around you and your mental chatter is not that loud.

Aside from learning how to enter a trance and recognize when you're in a trance, you must be familiar with how your mind receives psychic information. This is similar to things popping into your mind or you suddenly remembering something. Take note though, that it's easy to mistake psychic info with imagination, expectations, fears, desires, and the like, so you must start gathering info with a blank slate.

Focus on a target or ask a question. Wait for whatever comes into your mind. This can be anything – a memory, a sound, a voice, visuals, symbols, and more. Remember these and try to record them in some form through writing or describing them over a recorder.

When you notice that the stream of information starts to taper off, or if you suspect that you are just making it up already, stop recording. Look back at what you've gathered and try to interpret them. Record your interpretations as well. Afterwards, seek confirmation about whether your hunch is true or not.

Gradually, you will have a grasp of how your psychic abilities work and what certain signals mean. You will also learn how to distinguish false hunches from true ones.

You may already detect subtle energies, but if you want to sharpen this sense, you can practice by turning your focus inward and noticing how your mind portrays something to you. For example, if someone is really angry, notice what you're sensing. Are you seeing the color red in your mind's eye? Are you feeling heat on your skin? If there are a lot of children around, compare what you sense with when you're with elderly people. Soon, you will be able to learn your intuition's representations of the energies it detects.

Chapter 4. Consciously Controlling Empath Abilities

Learn the different energies by going into areas or immersing yourself in situations where those are present. You may also look at pictures, watch videos, or listen to songs that evoke them. This will make you work with emotions better, too.

The next chapter is all about chakras – energy centers along your body. You will be more ready to work with them when you have gained the ability to sense energy, but you can jump straight into the exercises if you want.

Chapter 5.

Chakra Development for Empaths

It's possible for an empath to have weakened chakras when they sacrifice too much for other people. Correcting these weakened chakras will help make things better for the empath. Take note that this is just a brief discussion of chakra development, and there are other things that are not included here such as yoga poses, chakra associations, dietary recommendations, and the likes. However, the information given below will be enough for most matters.

Root Chakra

The root chakra nestled at the base of the spine deals with survival, security, and physical existence. A sick root chakra brings fear, insecurity, and a lack of connectedness to earthly life, while a healthy root chakra brings strength, security, and a readiness to face life's challenges.

Physical tasks, especially those involving the legs and feet, help activate this chakra. Activities done in natural environments such as gardening and fishing will also be helpful.

Grounding involves connecting the root chakra with the energy of the earth. Focus on this chakra to regain your composure and stability in the midst of intense emotions. Red, earthy, or black crystals resonate to the root chakra's energies.

Sacral Chakra

The sacral chakra is stationed in the lower abdomen near the internal and external reproductive organs. It is linked to sexuality, creativity, pleasure, and sexual relationships. A disharmonious sacral chakra results to problems with the sex drive, guilt in achieving pleasure, addictions, or unhealthy relationships. When this chakra functions well, it enables fulfilling intimate connections and a balanced attitude towards pleasure.

Indulging in sensual, pleasurable experiences help soothe the sacral chakra. Doing these activities with a loving partner will be more effective in targeting the sacral chakra than being alone.

Because the sacral chakra is orange, orange crystals and gemstones may be used when focusing on this chakra. Focus here to improve your connections with those you are intimate with.

Solar Plexus Chakra

The solar plexus is within the abdomen and it's closely related to the digestive system because it absorbs energy and circulates it all throughout the energetic channels of the subtle body. The person's identity, ego, and will are solar plexus attributes.

Issues with the solar plexus shows up as extremes: powerlessness or dominance, an overinflated ego or lack of self-esteem. When the solar plexus is alright, the person is responsible with how he/she uses his/her own power, and he/she has a healthy self-esteem.

Effortful actions stimulate the solar plexus chakra because this is where a person's energy is centered. Examples of these are vigorous activities, competitive tasks, martial arts, and the likes.

Yellow crystals are best suited for solar plexus work. If you want to regain your sense of self and strengthen your boundaries, meditate on the solar plexus chakra.

Heart Chakra

The heart chakra serves as the energetic counterpart of the physical heart. It is believed to be the center where emotions are generated and felt.

When the heart chakra is blocked, the person may be having difficulties with processing emotions. He/she may also be prone to harboring negative feelings. When it is open, the chakra creates positive emotions and a love for one's self and for other people.

Clearing the heart chakra is done by doing things that evoke positive sentiments towards others, such as helping those in need, being with family and friends, or doing something enjoyable with other people.

Green colored gems are recommended for working with the heart chakra. To release negative emotions and attract positive ones, work on this chakra.

Throat Chakra

The throat chakra is linked to communication, expression, and the intellect. A weak throat chakra may be linked to difficulties in expressing one's self, lying, gossiping, overthinking or not thinking properly. A properly functioning throat chakra bestows good communication skills and clear thought.

Activities that balance the throat chakra are those that involve exercising one's thoughts and expressing them. Singing, reciting stories or poems, and other vocal exercises will also stimulate chakra.

Blue crystals are used for connecting to the throat chakra. Empaths may need to pay attention to this chakra because they tend to suppress their thoughts to prevent stirring up negative emotions around them.

Third Eye Chakra

The third eye chakra is between the two eyes deep within the head. It gives sight – both physical and clairvoyant sight. This chakra pertains to one's psychic abilities, abstract thought, and imagination.

A diseased third eye chakra may trigger mental difficulties, confusion, and inability to use psychic abilities. A strong third eye chakra enhances psychic abilities and strengthens the mind.

Meditation, contemplation, dream work, and mystical practices are some of the activities that can cleanse and empower the third eye chakra.

Indigo-colored or deep blue crystals resonate with the third eye chakra. A hyperactive third eye chakra may cause an empath's abilities to become overwhelming. If this is the case, visualizing one's third eye to slow down a bit may help control the symptoms.

Crown Chakra

The crown chakra is the highest of the major chakras. It symbolizes the unification of one's self to the Divine.

Spirituality, higher consciousness, and divine connection are the areas that pertain to the crown chakra.

Crown chakra imbalances may point to lack of spirituality, excessive materialism, and possibly insanity. When it is balanced, it gives spiritual fulfillment and a feeling of connectedness with the divine.

Spiritual acts such as dedicating one's life to God, sacrificing one's self for greater causes, and fervent praying can help purify the crown chakra.

Purple or white crystals are recommended for handling the crown chakra. Empaths usually have a strong crown chakra. If you think you need help from the spirit world, tap into the energies of this chakra.

Chapter 6 tackles a major challenge of being an empath: managing emotions. Although it is applicable to other people, it will matter to you a lot.

Chapter 6.

Emotional Management for Empaths

Empaths need to manage their emotions since they tend to feel more than the average person. Thankfully, there are a lot of techniques for achieving control over feelings regardless of how strong they seem to be.

Managing Undesirable Emotions

If you dislike how you feel, you can make it subside through the following methods:

Chapter 6. Emotional Management for Empaths

Calm Down

Emotions are a form of stimulation because they trigger changes in the body (example: fear causes the heart rate to speed up and increases muscle tension) and mind (emotions bring up thoughts and memories that are relevant to them). Calming down decreases this stimulation and weakens the impact of emotion.

Taking deep, slow, and even breaths is one easy way to calm down. Just as emotions affect how one breathes, deliberately controlling it will also affect what one feels. Notice what you feel and how you breathe. If you want to change your emotion, change your breathing pattern.

Another is to relax tense muscles – this will tell your brain that everything is alright so it will stop releasing hormones that trigger unpleasant sensations. Move around freely to affirm that you are free to do whatever you wish.

Stop entertaining aggravating thoughts and shift to relaxing thoughts. Bring up memories of you being peaceful and comfortable. You can also focus on something that you are looking forward to.

Change Your Perspective

What you feel is affected by how you think about the situation. If you change how you describe what's happening, or if you look at it from a different perspective, you will likewise change how you emotionally respond to it. For example, if someone is really angry, instead of blaming yourself like what empaths usually do, you can think that they're just feeling ill, so they can't help but release their frustration on others.

Focus On Your Priorities

There is simply no end to things that has the potential to bother you. You can do something about a few of them, while the rest are not within your power to control. If you try to control everything that happens to you, you'll just be more frustrated. However, your reaction to the things that happen to you are completely within your control.

What you focus on determines how you feel and think. If something demands your undivided attention, consider whether it's truly worth minding. The more of your energy that you spend for something, the less energy you will have for the things that are important. Because of this, you must decide what's worth focusing on and let go of the rest.

Fake the Emotion

The brain monitors the condition of the different parts of the body and it creates emotional responses based on what it senses. If your body language expresses a particular emotion, your brain will think that you are feeling the emotion, thus it will release hormones that will support it. As an example, grinning for at least three minutes will make a person happy even if he or she isn't really feeling upbeat. Making "power poses" such as standing with a wide stance and arms overhead will make a nervous person feel more self-assured. Pretend that you are already feeling your desired emotion and make your behavior reflect it. Soon enough, you will feel the emotion.

Process It

Thinking about whatever you're feeling will lessen its influence. This is because emotions are designed to be felt and acted upon. Thinking introduces additional factors to the process so it can potentially derail the process. It can also question the assumptions that support the emotions.

Emotions guide a person to do something in particular without having to think about it. If you think about the situation, you tell yourself that you intend to make a conscious choice, so the emotions may wane as it's not that necessary anymore.

Expressing It

Emotions are a form of energy because they are meant to propel the person into action. If you dislike the direction that your emotions are leading you towards, release it through a different way. You can use anger as a force to power you through a tedious chore, or you can turn sadness into a catalyst for touching poetry, for example. You can also write about what you feel or talk about it to someone who is willing to listen. This will help you review it more objectively.

Cultivating Positive Emotions

Being an empath makes one vulnerable to negativities such as:

- Anger

- Resentment

- Disgust

- Anxiety

- Fear

- Grief

- Guilt

- Insecurity

- Feeling Overwhelmed

- Feeling Helpless

- Internal Conflict

Because you are extra-sensitive to emotions, it's healthier if you stop holding on to negative emotions and gravitate more to positive ones. The more often you do this, the more natural it will be to you until it becomes part of your normal, everyday "aura".

Aside from the techniques mentioned about, you can let go of unpleasant emotions through the following methods:

Chapter 6. Emotional Management for Empaths

- Leaving the cause or trigger of the emotion

- Visualizing the emotions as fading into nothingness

- Exercising

- Creating affirmations and reciting them regularly

- Doing something enjoyable and fulfilling

- Staying with people who make you happy

- Labeling emotions so you can consider it for what it is instead of just feeling it

- Relabeling the emotion into something more positive (example: fear into excitement, anger into motivation, sadness into cherishing)

- Meditating

- Observing whatever you feel in a detached manner

- Reminding yourself that you are not your emotions and they will soon pass

- Focusing more on things and thoughts that foster positive feelings

- Pretending the emotion is a person and talking to it to know it's message

- Thanking the emotion for its help

- Viewing the emotion in a more positive light

- Reminding yourself of good things about the feeling or thing that is bothering you

- Finding out the purpose of the emotion and doing something about it

Emotions are tools that are meant to help us act on things. Don't let them use you but learn to use them instead. Once you do, not only will you survive being an empath, you will even be someone who can empower other people.

Chapter 7.

A Toolbox of Techniques for the Empath

These are some of the best tools that an empath will most likely need. Although the main challenge of being an empath is learning how to have better emotional management, this chapter deals with more specific issues that are also as important as handling emotions well.

Deal With Indecisiveness

Take time in deciding for as long as the situation allows it. Ask for more time if you really need to think things over, and if you can afford to wait longer. Pretend that you have already decided upon something. This will change your mood, and your perspective will follow. This will allow you to see things more clearly so you can decide more easily.

Reduce the Risk of being Drained

These are situations where it's likely that you will be drained:

- Being obsessed

- Excessively talked to

- Trying to be accepted

- Feeling guilty

- Being a martyr

- Forcing yourself or being forced to act unnaturally

- Interacting with someone who is dishonest or hiding something

- Being taken advantage of

- Having loveless relationships

- Drama

- Being abused

- Someone depending on you too much

- Being controlled

- Feeling unwelcome

- Being insecure

- Feeling unsafe

- Trying hard to fit in/be accepted

- Experiencing Chronic Fatigue or other illnesses

Chapter 7. A Toolbox of Techniques for the Empath

Pay attention to situations when you feel uncomfortable or depleted. Whenever you encounter these again, ask yourself if you really need to go through it. If yes, defend yourself using the techniques you've learned in this book. If no, forget about it or pass it on to another person.

Set Limits and Boundaries

You must have a firm idea of who you are, what your priorities are, what your goals are and what you want to do. Using these ideas, set boundaries and do not let people push them.

Always remember that there are times when people do not really need you but they will just take advantage of your caring nature. Some may even enjoy seeing you do so much without asking for anything in return. Take care of yourself first and foremost. You are responsible for your own wellbeing.

Only help when it's really needed and when doing so will not harm you. If you notice that a person has become dependent on you, be kind by letting him/her stand on his/her own feet. It may feel good to be needed but you are just making both of you weak.

Stop Being a Martyr

Stop feeling guilty about things that you don't really need to feel guilty for. Guilt is an energy drain. Believe that whatever you did or did not do has some beneficial effect to others and to yourself.

Cease worrying too much about other people. Although you know you can help them, if they don't ask for help, it's likely that they don't need help at all. There are things that they have to resolve for themselves for their own personal growth.

Ask yourself, are you concerned about others because you want to feel needed and important?

Is it also possible that you want to control the other person but you don't want to appear mean, so you disguise it as helping? Being honest with yourself will free you from patterns of unhealthy behaviors.

Develop a Strong Identity

Empathizing so much with other people can make your identity changeable. This may result from wanting to please other people or to make them feel they are not alone. This may earn you some friends for the short term, but they will eventually mistrust you when they notice that you keep on changing depending on who you're with.

Keep in mind that people will be fine without you modifying yourself to please them. They will appreciate a person who is consistent rather than someone who fakes things to gain approval. Also, if they want you to think and act a certain way, they don't really care about you but they just want to manipulate you. Don't give them that chance – you are just encouraging them to be abusive not only to you but perhaps to others as well.

Build Self Confidence

An empath will be aware when people around them do not have pleasant thoughts and feelings about them. This makes an empath become more prone to developing insecurities than those who are oblivious to others' reactions towards them. Because of this, empaths may develop social anxieties and feel bad about themselves, always blaming themselves for not being accepted in a group.

If you're having problems with your self-esteem, remember that nobody is perfect, and nobody has to be. Learn to accept yourself for who you are despite what others think about you. You don't need to feel bad when they don't know who you really are or don't like you if you know and like yourself. Remember – even if they can affect how you feel, you can change how you feel too. Choose to feel good.

Choose Your Company

Surround yourself with people who support you. Be objective and specify who in your social circles are not that pleasant towards you. Stay away from them even if you feel attached to them. A little distance may make you see them in a more truthful light.

When people want to leave the relationship, don't hold on to them. Those who love and accept you will stay, while those who don't will naturally drift away from you. You don't have to change who you are just to keep them around. Even if very few remain, they are those who are worth your company.

Don't be afraid to disappoint or let go of people. You can get over whatever negative emotions that will be involved, but if you keep appeasing them, you will just prolong your agony. Whatever happens, consider it as something that will contribute to spiritual growth.

Don't Take Too Much Responsibilities

Even if you feel emotionally compelled to help someone or do things, you must protect yourself so you won't stretch yourself thin. This is especially important if you have grown so used to being kind.

As an empath, you may be compelled to help others more than necessary because you feel their negative emotions. However, always remember that you are not them, and it's possible that you are stopping them from maturing because you do things that they are supposed to do themselves. Sometimes, you also have to let them face the consequences of their actions or deal with unpleasant emotions so they will become stronger people.

People may resent you for not helping them as you usually do, but in the end, your feelings are yours and their feelings are theirs. If you want to help others, set limits as to how and when you will do this. Don't let it interfere with how you want to live your life. After all, it's your life, not theirs.

Express Yourself

Empaths are so used to absorbing emotions of those around them that they also tend to keep in what they really feel. They do not want to bother others because that will bother them too! However, once you learn how to separate your own self from other people, you will take care of yourself better. One of the first steps of doing that is to know what's really in your heart and say it openly. Not everyone is an empath like you. You need to spell it out for them.

Remember: everyone and everything is connected, and you as an empath can feel this connection more than anyone else. However, you are still you so your prime responsibility is yourself. Help when you can, but be merciful to yourself. We can only give what we have. Nourish yourself so you will have plenty to share.

Conclusion

Being an empath means being capable of sensing and giving more than the ordinary person. Whatever you decide to do with your gift is ultimately your decision, but may it be something that will help you grow as an individual. Not everyone is like you and not everyone can do what you can. Because of this, try to use your gifts in ways that will benefit humanity, or at least those who are close to you.

Most importantly, never lose sight of yourself despite having a wider perspective than normal. Although you may feel others more strongly, what's inside you matters, too. Once you've taken care of yourself, you will be more capable of serving others. Let them help you, too – being kind feels nice.

We are all linked to each other whether this is felt or not. As one who feels this deeply, you have

Conclusion

the most potential to benefit from this connection. May this fill you with joy and courage.

Once again, don't forget to grab a copy of your FREE BONUS book *"The Secrets Behind Subtle Psychology: Secrets To Getting All You Want"*. If you are interested in learning more about human psychology and being more effective in conversations, then this book is for you.

Just go to http://bit.ly/subtlepsychology

Lastly, if you enjoyed reading the book, could you please take time to share your views with us by posting a review on Amazon? Having a positive review from you helps the book stay on top of the ranks, so we can continue to reach those who can benefit from the information shared within the book. It'd be highly appreciated!

To your success.